Project 7-11

Moving on in Science

Godfrey Hall

for 9-10 year olds

Letts

1 How hard is it?

Many metals are bright and shiny and they will allow electricity to pass through them easily. Metals are difficult to break but they can be beaten into other shapes or pulled out into wire.

You can test metals by scratching them with objects of different hardness.

You will need:
- an old, blunt knife
- a magnifying glass
- a milk bottle top
- a nail
- a coin
- a stone

▶ Look round your house and garden.

▶ Write down in your notebook how many things you can find that are made of metal.

Are any of the drinks cans made of aluminium? Do you know why this is?

▶ Try to scratch the blade of an old, blunt knife with a pencil. What do you notice?

▶ Now scratch it with a nail. Look at this through your magnifying glass.

What do you see?

Do you notice any difference between the pencil mark scratch and the nail scratch?

▶ Now test the aluminium milk bottle top in the same way. Do you notice any differences?

▶ Find some other objects to test.

You could use a coin, a stone, a brick...

▶ Find some more scratchers like a piece of chalk, a piece of metal, a piece of concrete, a piece of coal.

▶ Try the scratch test on the objects using your different scratchers.

▶ Fill in the chart below with your results.

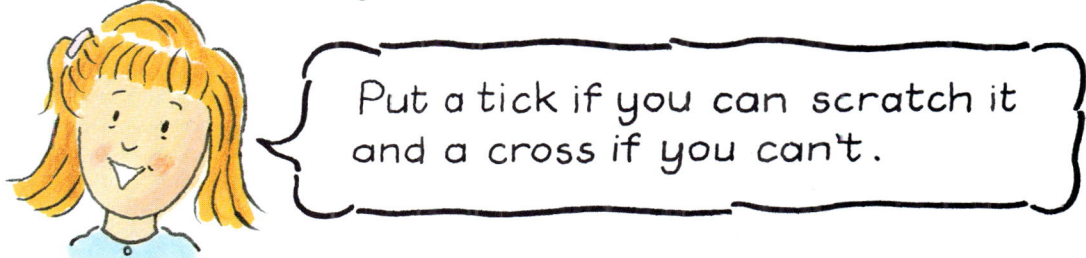

Put a tick if you can scratch it and a cross if you can't.

Scratchers	Objects				
	Coin	Old knife	Bottle top	Nail	Stone
Chalk					
Metal					
Concrete					
Wood					
Coal					

Which do you think was the hardest item that you scratched?

▶ Mark them from 1 to 5 in order of hardness.

▶ Now do the same with the scratchers.

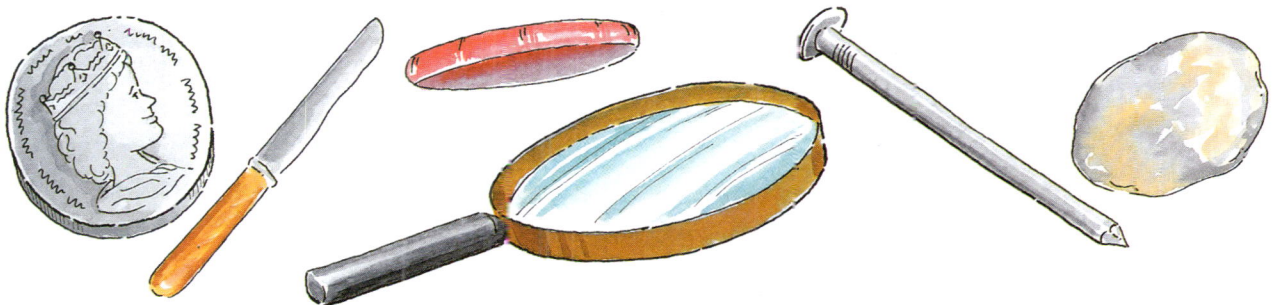

2 Touch, taste and smell

"Let's see what other games we can play using a blindfold."

"Don't tie the blindfold too tight!"

You will need:
- a selection of small objects
- a tray
- a scarf or large handkerchief
- different coins
- fruit gums
- a little coffee, tea, vinegar
- a slice of lemon, onion
- some containers, e.g. plastic cups

▶ Blindfold someone and then put ten different items on a tray in front of them.

▶ Ask them to feel the items and then to tell you what they are.
How many did they guess right the first time?

"You could use a spoon, a cup, a screwdriver, a rubber..."

▶ Blindfold someone else and put some different coins on the table in front of them.

▶ Ask them to guess the value of each coin by feeling it. Apart from the size was there anything else that helped them to find out what it was?

▶ Now collect together some different types of material. Ask the person who has been blindfolded to put them in order, starting with the smoothest.

▶ Another idea would be to give the blindfolded person pieces of string of different lengths and get them to put them in order of length.

Can you think up any other games that use touch?

▶ Get a packet of fruit gums.

▶ Blindfold a friend.

▶ Put one of each flavour in front of them.
Let them taste each one.
Can they guess the flavour of each sweet?

Which ones did they get right?

I like the fruit gums test!

You could try the same test out on someone else and compare the results.

Were any of the flavours difficult to recognize?

Another test you could do is one using smell. Make sure you do this in the kitchen by the sink!

You will need some coffee, tea, lemon, onion and vinegar.

▶ Put a small amount of each into a container such as a plastic cup.

▶ Blindfold someone and let them have a sniff at each one.

▶ Write down in the space below what they think the smells are.

Substance	Guess	Were they right?
Coffee		
Tea		
Lemon		
Onion		
Vinegar		

Can you think of other foods you could try?

You could also try out this test using a selection of different fruits such as an orange, banana, pear, grape and apple.

3 Seed tests

You will need:
- a plastic egg box
- marrow seeds
- sunflower seeds
- bean or pea seeds
- apple pips
- a medicine dropper
- a plastic bag
- 2 flower pots
- 2 straws

▶ Number each section of your egg box from 1 to 6.

▶ Fill the box with soil, making sure each compartment is full.

▶ Put a marrow seed into each section. Water each of your seeds using the chart below.

Section	How much water
1	No water at all
2	One drop a day
3	Two drops a day
4	Three drops a day
5	Four drops a day
6	Five drops a day

▶ Put your egg box garden into a clear, plastic bag and put it somewhere light and warm. Watch what happens over the next two weeks.

Remember to water your seeds every day (except for number 1).

What kinds of seeds grow the quickest?

To find out, try growing some different types of seeds in your egg box garden.

Do you think the biggest seeds will be the fastest growers?

Will the longest seeds make the tallest plants?

▶ Once the seeds have germinated, pick the two strongest seedlings and replant them into two flower pots. Make sure you handle them carefully.

▶ Stick in a straw by the side of each seedling.

▶ Every other day measure them against the straws and fill in the chart below.

Day	Height in centimetres	
	Seed 1	Seed 2
1		
3		
5		
7		
9		
11		
13		
15		

Do you think it will make any difference which way up the seeds are planted?

Try planting some seeds upside down and recording what happens in your notebook.

You could also try planting your seeds in different things such as shredded newspaper, sand and sawdust.

Where do your plants grow best?

4 Making yoghurt

You will need:
- a saucepan
- 1 pint (570ml) full-fat milk
- a clean jug
- a tablespoon of live yoghurt
- 1 pint thermos flask
- a tub of plain, full-fat yoghurt
- a rubber band
- a large bowl
- a piece of clean cloth

Yoghurt is made from milk which is sterilized by heating it. The mixture is then cooled, a special bacteria is added and then it is warmed again.

 **Warning** You will need an adult to help you.

Here is how to make your own yoghurt.

▶ Pour the milk into the pan.

▶ **With an adult**, heat it very slowly, almost to boiling point, making sure that it doesn't boil.

- ▶ **Ask an adult** to pour it into the thermos flask.
- ▶ Add a tablespoon of the live yoghurt. Stir the mixture gently.
- ▶ Screw on the top of the thermos. Leave it somewhere warm for two days.
  When it is opened up you should have some thick yoghurt.

Do you know why the milk has turned into yoghurt?

You could add some jam to your yoghurt to flavour it.

Did you know that by using some plain yoghurt, it is possible to make your own cheese?

Mmm!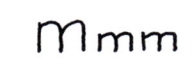

- ▶ Pour out the plain yoghurt carefully on to the cloth. Make it into a bag shape by pulling the ends of the cloth tight.
- ▶ Fasten the top of the bag with the rubber band. Hang the bag over the bowl for three or four days until it has stopped dripping.
- ▶ Unwrap the bag carefully and put your cheese into the bowl.

What does it look like now?
How has the yoghurt changed?

Why do you think this has happened?

Does it taste good?
See if you can improve the taste by adding a little salt or butter.

 *We put ours on some toast!*

5 Time to stop

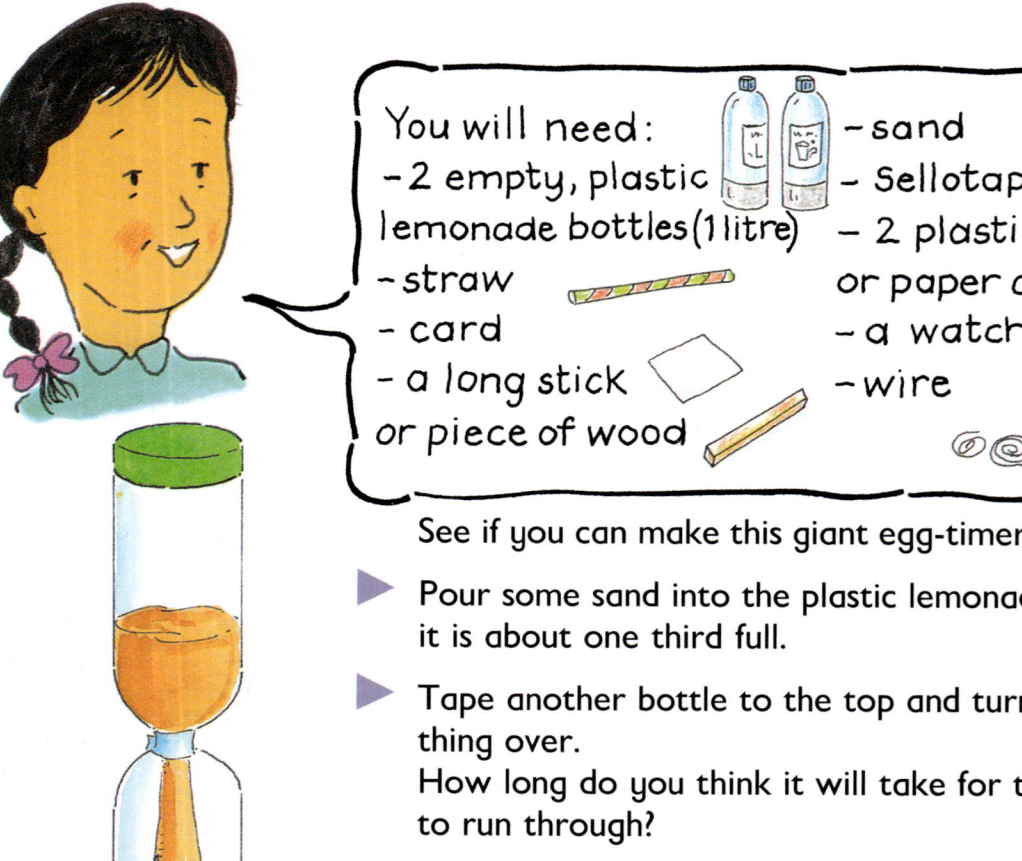

See if you can make this giant egg-timer.

▶ Pour some sand into the plastic lemonade bottle until it is about one third full.

▶ Tape another bottle to the top and turn the whole thing over.
How long do you think it will take for the sand to run through?

How can you make the sand flow slower or faster?

▶ Try out other materials instead of sand such as salt, water or thin flour paste.
Which are quicker or slower than the sand?

Does changing the size of the hole in between the two bottles make a difference to how it works?

See if you can make a timer that times for exactly one minute.

Do this near a sink!

▶ Using two plastic cups, a long stick and some card see if you can design your own water timer.

Below is one design you might like to use.

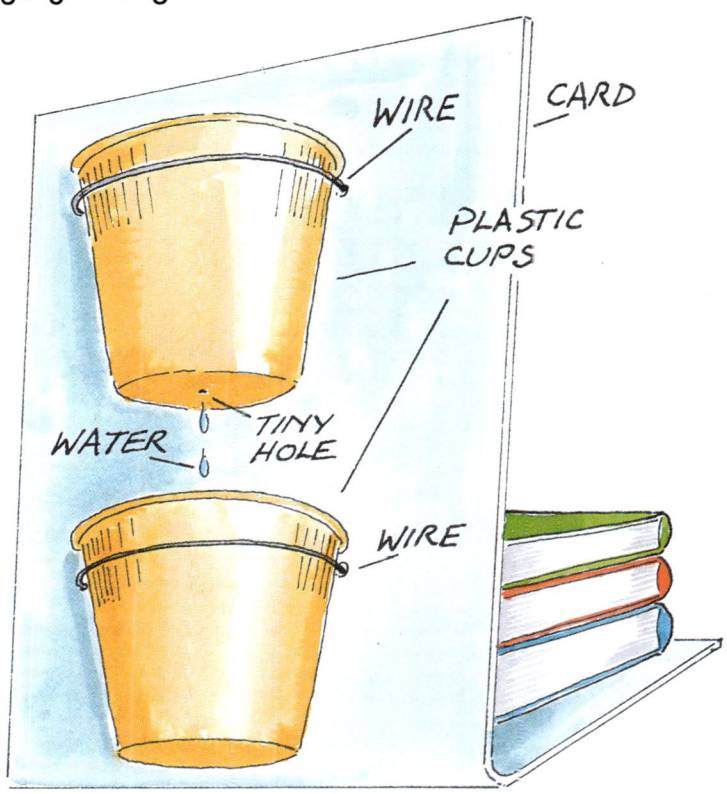

What else could you use instead of water? Will you need more or less of this for your minute timer? Why is this?

Check how accurate your timer is by using a watch to time how long the water takes to drop from the bottom to the top.

6 Engine power

"This is good fun. I wonder what other kinds of boats we could make."

You will need:
- a piece of balsa or soft wood
- a rubber band
- 2 tacks or drawing pins
- a lolly stick
- Plasticine
- a piece of paper

There are many different ways to make a boat move across the water.

Warning

▶ **Get an adult** to cut a boat shape out of your piece of wood.

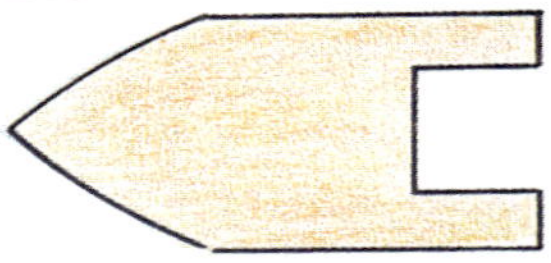

▶ Put the boat into a sink or bowl of water. Give it a push and watch how it moves. Where did the energy come from to move your boat?

See if you can make a paper sail for your boat.

▶ Fix it on to the boat with the Plasticine and gently blow the sail. Does your sail improve the way it moves across the water?

▶ Design a different kind of sail for your boat and try it out. Which of your designs is the most successful?

Another way of making your boat move is to give it an engine.

Here is one simple way to make an engine.

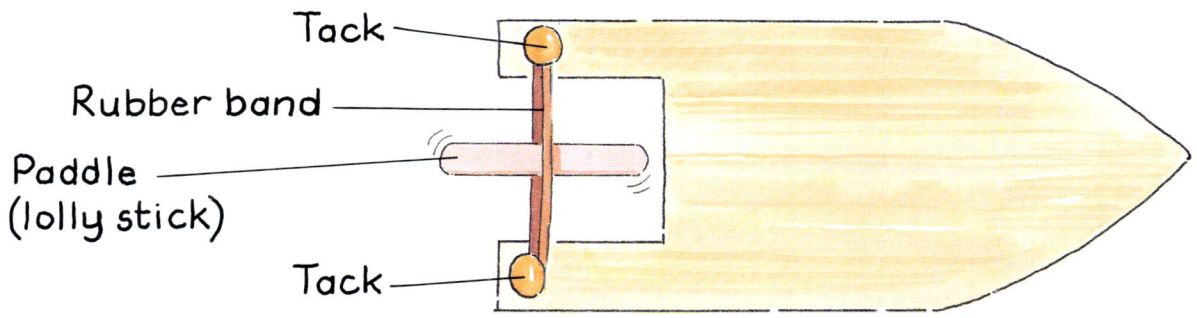

- Bang two tacks or drawing pins into your boat shape, as shown.
- Fix the rubber band to the tacks.
- Carefully cut your lolly stick to make a paddle and put it between the rubber band.
- Wind the paddle around until it is tight.
- Put your paddle boat into the water and let it go. Watch how it moves across the water. Does it go forwards or backwards?

> Does it work better with an extra paddle?

Can you make it go further by increasing the thickness of the rubber band?

Does the number of turns of the rubber band make a difference to how far it goes?

- Fill in this chart.

Number of turns	Distance travelled (in centimetres)

7 Water beasts

Land creatures and those that live in water often move in different ways.

What kind of differences can you think of in the way that they move? Jot them down in your notebook.

Here is one way that you can look at water creatures more closely.

Remember this is only a short-term home. You must return the creatures back to their homes after one or two weeks.

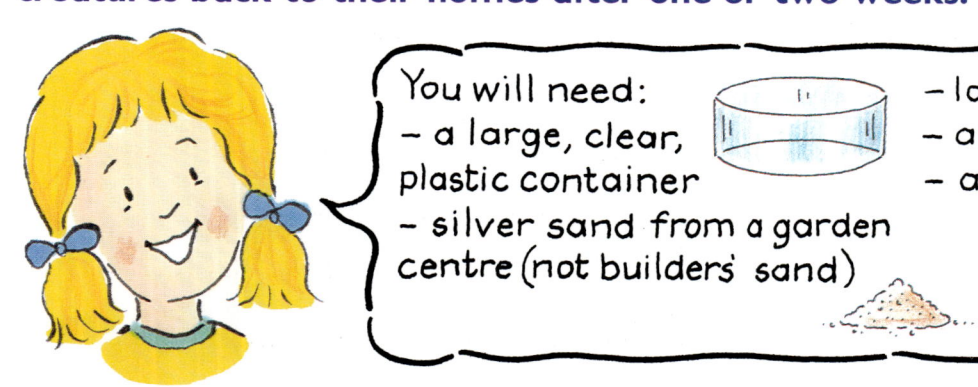

You will need:
- a large, clear, plastic container
- silver sand from a garden centre (not builders' sand)
- large, clean stones
- a net
- a large jar

▶ Wash out your container or tank.

▶ Put in a layer of sand 5cm deep. Add some clean stones.

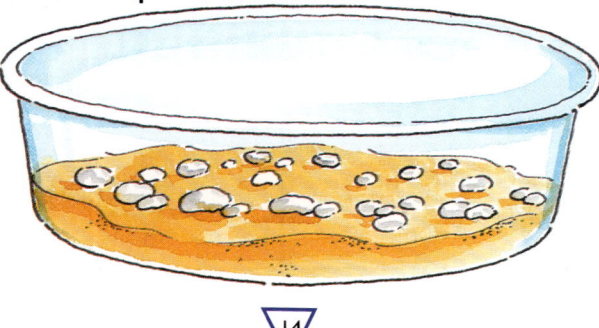

Make sure that you have an adult with you.

▶ Take your net and go along to a local pond.

Before you collect your creatures for your water home, look at them in the water and watch how they move.

What kind of creatures are on the surface of the pond? Make a list of them in your notebook.

What happens to the creatures if the water is disturbed in any way?

▶ Put some pond water and some pond weed in a large jar.

▶ Transfer your creatures to the jar. Take them back to the tank and put them into the water **very carefully**.

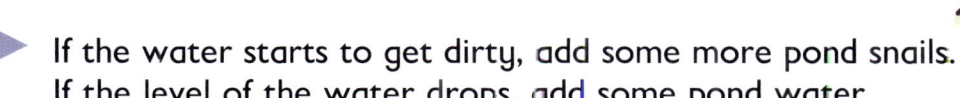

Make sure you put your tank somewhere safe and away from the window.

▶ If the water starts to get dirty, add some more pond snails. If the level of the water drops, add some pond water.

You might need to put a lid on your container, but do make sure that there are some holes in it.

▶ Look carefully at the creatures you have collected. Do any of the creatures' parts move when they are still?

See if you can find some garden snails. How are they different from your pond snails?

Think about their colour and shapes and the way they move.

▶ Draw a pond snail and a garden snail in the box below showing the differences between them.

8 Changing shapes

You will need:
- a torch
- card
- a pair of scissors
- white paper
- a needle and cotton

▶ Darken a room and shine a torch on to the wall.

▶ Put your hand into the beam of light and see what kinds of shapes or patterns you can make on the wall.

By moving your hands can you make the shapes bigger and smaller?

Does your hand have to be nearer the wall or the torch to make the shape bigger?

▶ Cut out a circle, a square and a rectangle from a piece of card.

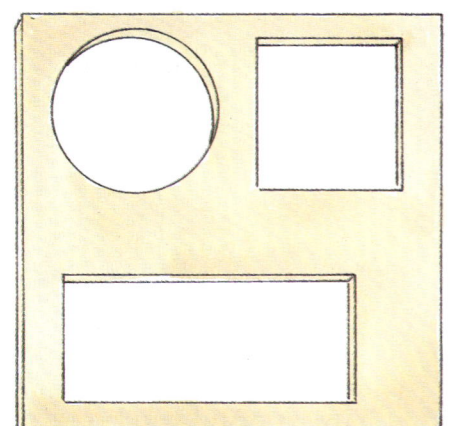

▶ Thread the cotton through the shapes so that you can dangle them.

▶ Put the square into the beam of light and watch what happens to the shadow as you turn it. Can you make the shadow change shape?

Does moving the torch nearer to the card make any difference to the shadow on the wall?

Try moving the torch to the left and the right of the square.

▶ Now try out other shapes.

▶ Draw in your notebook some of the shapes you can make by moving the torch to the left or the right.

▶ Put a piece of white paper on a table. Place a small object on the paper.

▶ Shine the torch so that the beam of the light casts a shadow on the paper.

What do you notice about the shadow as you move the torch further back? What happens if you move it closer to the object?

▶ Draw the shadow on the piece of paper.

▶ Now see if you can make your own shadow puppet theatre using different shaped cards of figures and objects.

> You could invite some friends around to a puppet show!

Where do you have to position the light to get the best effect?

9 Making windmills

Fuels such as coal and oil are being used up and people are looking for different ways to produce energy. One way is using wind power.

Are there any old windmills near you?

When were they built?

Here is one way to make a simple windmill of your own.

You will need:
- a bead
- a thin cane
- a pair of scissors
- thin card
- a strong pin
- 4 yoghurt pots
- 2 garden canes or a long, thin piece of wood
- a nail

▶ Cut out a square of card with sides 16cm long.

▶ Draw two lines from corner to corner.

▶ Cut halfway along each line towards the middle of the card.

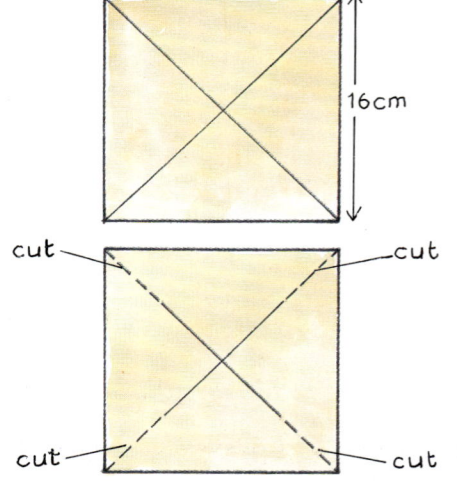

▶ **1** Take the corners marked A, B, C and D and **2** bend them over into the centre.

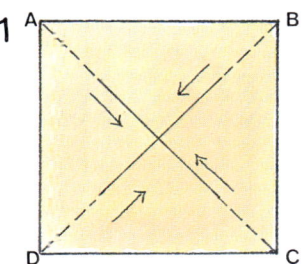 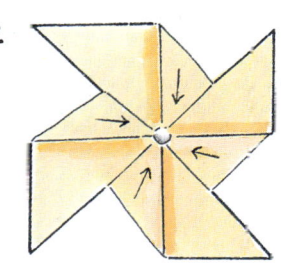

▶ Put the bead between the card and the stick.

▶ Put the pin through the card and the bead and push it into the stick.

▶ Blow it or take it outside in the wind. Can you improve the design in any way?

▶ A different sort of windmill can be made by fitting four empty yoghurt pots on to two crossed sticks.

▶ Fit these on to another stick with a nail as shown.

Warning **You will need an adult to help you with this.**

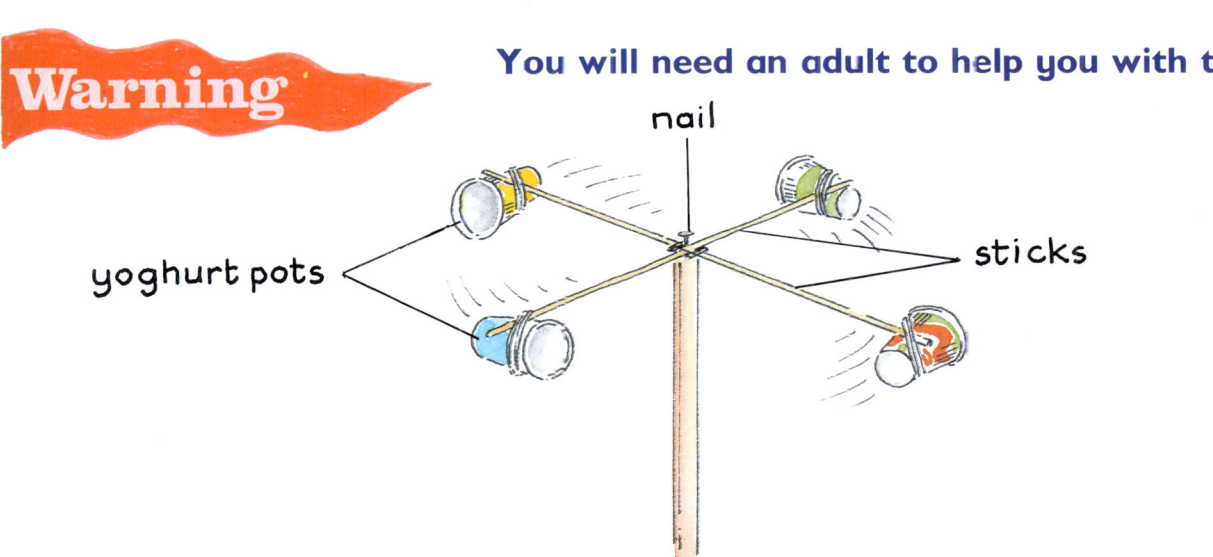

Which of your windmills is the best?

Do the yoghurt pots rotate faster or slower when the wind blows?

10 Does it dissolve?

"One sugar, please!"

You will need:
- 1 level teaspoon of
  - salt
  - flour
  - washing powder
- sugar
- dried milk
- custard powder
- a jug
- a clear cup

▶ When you add each powder to the water write down what you think will happen in the chart on the opposite page.

▶ Take a clean jug and half fill it with water.

▶ Add a level teaspoon of one of the powders.

▶ Watch what happens as you add the powder.

▶ Record your results in the chart opposite.

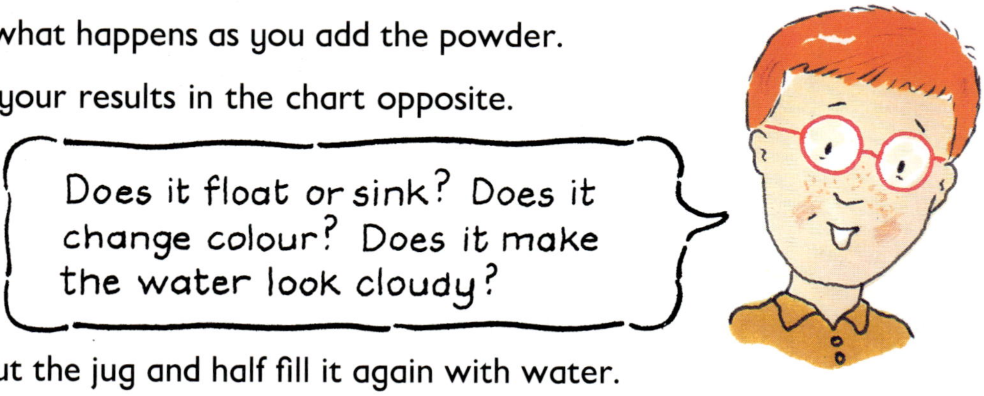

"Does it float or sink? Does it change colour? Does it make the water look cloudy?"

▶ Wash out the jug and half fill it again with water.

▶ Add another powder.

Make sure you use the same amount of water each time.

Do this until you have finished testing all the powders.

Powder	What I think will happen	What actually happens
Salt		
Flour		
Washing powder		
Sugar		
Dried milk		
Custard powder		

▶ Try collecting together some other substances.

▶ Watch what happens when they are put into water.

> You could try a piece of chalk, a sugar cube, a stock cube...

▶ In the box below write down a list of things around your house that might dissolve in water and those things that might not.

▶ Try your tests again using **warm** water from the tap.

Is there any difference in your results? Why do you think this is?

Does it make any difference if you stir the powders?

▶ Find out how fast some things dissolve by taking a teaspoonful of each powder and putting it in a cup half filled with water.

▶ Time how long it takes to disappear.

11 Lifting with levers

You will need:
- some nails
- a block of wood deeper than the nails
- a claw hammer

Levers are simple devices that will move objects. They were used by people over 100,000 years ago before the wheel was invented.

Stone Age people used levers to lift heavy rocks and stones that they could not lift alone.

Today we use levers to move all sorts of different things.

Pulling out nails with a hammer...

...or taking the lid off something with a coin.

Warning 🚩 **Ask an adult to help.**

▶ Bang some nails into the piece of wood using the hammer.

▶ Leave the heads of the nails sticking out slightly.

▶ Hold the hammer half-way up the handle and try to pull out one of the nails.

▶ Now try pulling out another nail holding the end of the hammer.

Which is easier?

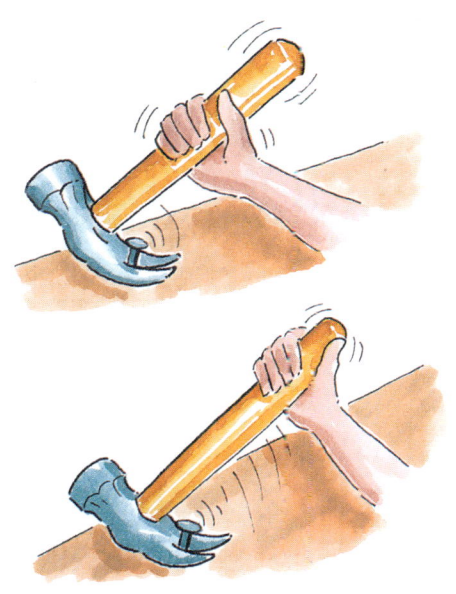

Although it doesn't look like a lever, a wheelbarrow works in the same way.

It helps you to carry heavier loads than you can move alone.

This is because the handles are further away from the balancing point (the wheel) than the load.

A see-saw is another kind of lever.

▶ Go to the park with your family or friends and find out how one person can lift two or more people sitting at the other end of a see-saw.

▶ Make a list in your notebook of some of the different ways levers are used, eg to work brakes and signals.

12 Papermaking

▶ Collect together some different types of paper.

▶ Look at the paper closely and see if you can spot any differences.

Is the paper easy to tear?

Does it all feel the same?

Making your own paper can be great fun ... **but** it can be very messy. Make sure that you do this outside or in the kitchen.

You will need:
- different types of paper
- an old shirt or apron
- an ice cream lid
- an old pair of tights
- lots of newspaper
- paper towels
- powder paint (for coloured paper)
- a hand whisk
- a washing-up bowl
- a rolling pin
- an old tablespoon
- some clean cloth
- ½ bucket of warm water

▶ Put on an old shirt or apron.

▶ **Stage 1**

Cut 5 or 6 holes in your lid.

Cut a piece out of a pair of tights and stretch it over the lid.
Make sure there are lots of holes in the tights!

This is called the **mould** and **deckle**.

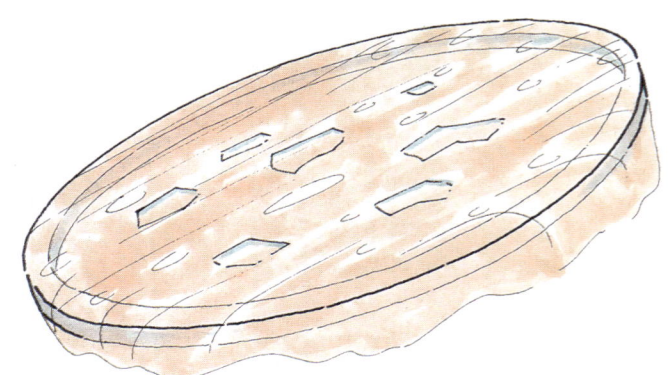

▶ **Stage 2**

Tear up the newspaper into tiny pieces. Put them into your bucket of warm water.

(If you want coloured paper, add 4 tablespoons of powder paint to the water before putting in the paper.)

Mash it up into a pulp.

Leave it for about 2 hours until it becomes very soft.

▶ **Stage 3**

Pour away any excess water.

Mash up the paper again using your hands, then whisk it into a pulp.

Tip the pulp into the washing-up bowl.

Put the paper towel on to a piece of newspaper next to the bowl.

Take your mould and dip it into the bowl. Slide it under the surface.

Lift it up carefully, making sure you have a layer of pulp on the lid.

Let any water drain back into the bowl.

▶ **Stage 4**

Turn your mould upside down. Let the pulp fall on to the paper.

Put another piece of paper towel on the top.

Roll your rolling pin over the top to squeeze out even more water.

Peel off the paper towel from the top.

Leave the paper in a warm place to dry. It will take about 2 days.

When it is dry peel off the bottom layer of paper towel.

Decorate your paper using paints or felt tips.

Does the paper soak up your colours?

13 The night sky

You will need:
- a pair of binoculars or a telescope
- a book on stars

▶ Look out of the window on a clear night or go outside **with an adult** when it is dark.

▶ Look through your telescope or binoculars and, in the box, draw a sketch of the moon.

▶ Do the same thing each week for one month and draw what you see each time.

Week	Shape of moon
One	
Two	
Three	
Four	

The moon circles the earth about every 28 days. It is a waterless, airless place and is covered with a large number of craters.

When the moon is full the sun is shining straight on to the side that is facing the earth.

When there is a new moon the sun is behind the moon and shining on the other side.

If the moon is shaped like this it's called a **crescent** moon.

If it is like this it is called a **full** moon.

Many of the small points of light you can see in the night sky are stars. These are millions of miles away.

Some of the points of light are called planets. There are nine of these in our solar system.

▶ Find out their names and write them in the space below.

If you go out when it is just getting dark, on a very clear night, you may catch a glimpse of the planet Venus. It can be seen as a very bright point of light in the evening sky.

14 Light it up

"What do you think we could use these for?"

You will need:
- a torch bulb
- a bulb holder
- a battery
- 90 cm of covered wire
- 2 drawing pins
- paper clips
- a small block of soft wood
- a pair of snippers

Remember: electricity can be dangerous. Never play with anything connected to the main supply.

Using the things listed above can you make a bulb light up?

Some materials will let electricity flow through them. These are called **conductors**. Others will stop the flow of electricity. These are called **insulators**.

▶ Collect together some different items from around the house such as a metal spoon, a wooden spoon and a plastic pen top.

▶ Fill in the chart opposite to show which are conductors and which are insulators.

"Do you know why?"

Choose some objects yourself and add them to the list.

Object	Conductor	Insulator
Metal spoon Wooden spoon Pen top Paper clip		

Can you make your light flash by a simple switch?

Here is one idea.

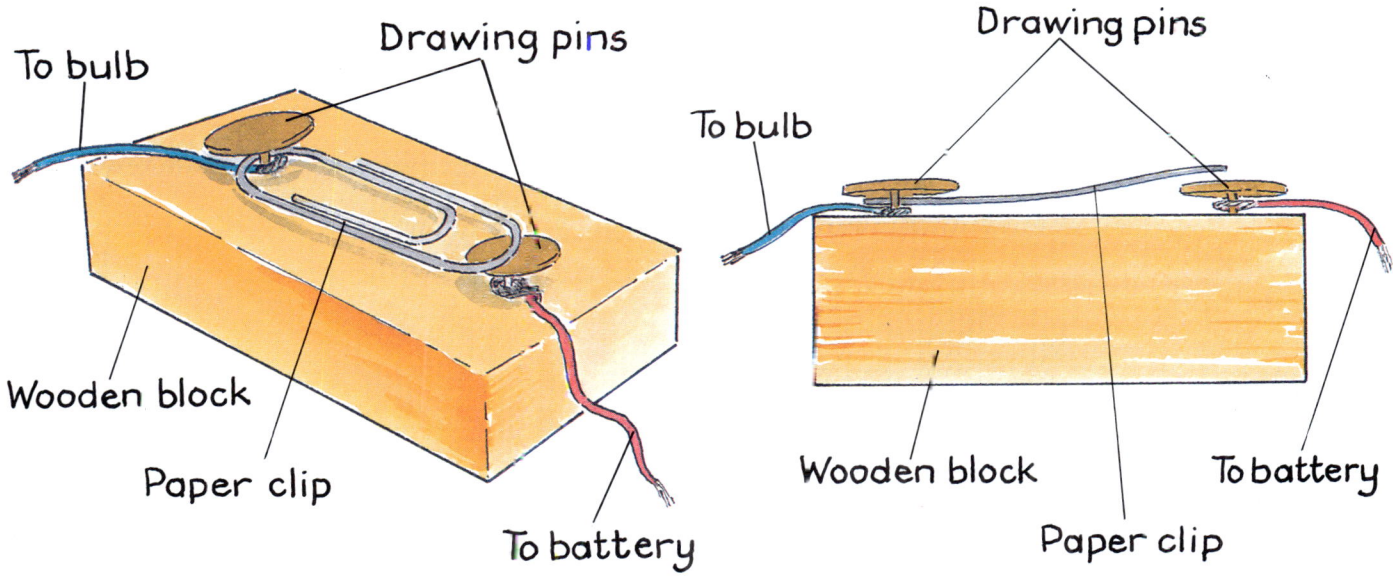

- See if you can make any other types of switches to turn your light on and off.

What else could you fix into your circuit instead of a bulb?

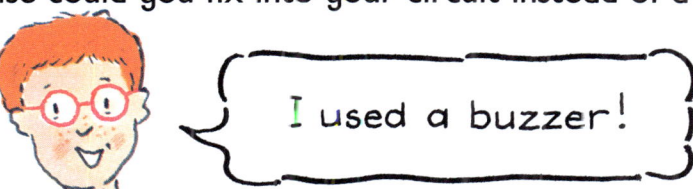

I used a buzzer!

You could make up your own code.

- Using a shoe box, see if you can use your light and switch as part of a model room, or even a lighthouse.

Another idea might be to use your circuit for flashing secret messages.

15 Where do they live?

You will need:
- a magnifying glass
- a book on plants
- a book on minibeasts
- a hoop or cardboard frame

▶ Go into the garden or park and find an open space.

▶ Throw down your hoop or frame.

▶ Look closely and carefully at the plants and creatures inside your frame.

   Remember: do not disturb them!

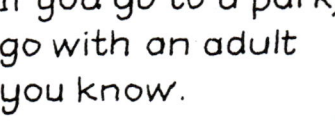

▶ Find two or three plants and sketch them in your notebook. **Do not pick them.**

▶ See if you can find any creatures. Sketch these as well.

▶ Try the same thing under a tree. Are there any differences in what you find?

▶ When you get home see if you can identify some of the plants and minibeasts from your reference books.

Did you find any man-made objects in the space?
Were they made of paper, wood, plastic or something else?

Think about how they came to be there.

▶ Make a list of natural and man-made objects that you found.
Put a tick in the correct column in the chart below.

Object	Natural	Man-made
Paper Wood Plastic Glass		

Guess how long it would take, if you left them where you found them, before they would rot away.

Would it be a day, a month, a year, hundreds of years, never …?

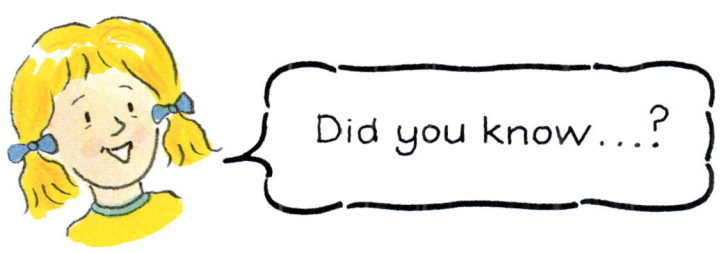

Did you know…?

About 4.5 billion drinks cans are thrown away in Britain each year. If they were placed end to end they would reach the moon.

Each year the paper and board that we throw away equals two trees for every person.

Each person also throws away 45kg of plastics every year.

So remember: think before you throw!

Chart showing National Curriculum attainment targets together with topics covered

	Exploration of science	Variety of life	Processes of life	Genetics and evolution	Human influence on earth	Types and uses of materials	Making new materials	How materials behave	Earth and atmosphere	Forces	Electricity and magnetism	Information technology	Energy	Sound and music	Light/electromagnetic radiation	Earth in space	Nature of science
How hard is it?	●					●											
Touch, taste and smell	●			●													
Seed tests	●	●	●	●													
Making yoghurt	●					●	●	●									
Time to stop	●									●							
Engine power	●									●			●				
Water beasts	●	●	●	●													
Changing shapes	●														●		
Making windmills	●									●			●				
Does it dissolve?	●					●											
Lifting with levers	●									●			●				
Papermaking	●					●											
The night sky	●															●	
Light it up	●										●						
Where do they live?	●	●															